GEOMETRIC PATTERNS AND DESIGNS
for Artists and Craftspeople

Wil Stegenga

DOVER PUBLICATIONS, INC.
Mineola, New York

Copyright

Copyright © 2002 by Wil Stegenga
All rights reserved under Pan American and International Copyright Conventions.

Published in the United Kingdom by David & Charles, Brunel House, Forde Close, Newton Abbot, Devon TQ12 4PU.

Bibliographical Note

Geometric Patterns and Designs for Artists and Craftspeople is a new work, first published by Dover Publications, Inc., in 2002.

DOVER *Pictorial Archive* SERIES

Library of Congress Cataloging-in-Publication Data

Stegenga, Wil.
    Geometric patterns and designs for artists and craftspeople / Wil Stegenga.
        p. cm. — (Dover pictorial archive series)
    ISBN 0-486-42308-5 (pbk.)
    1. Repetitive patterns (Decorative arts) I. Title. II. Series.

NK1570 .S73 2002
745.4—dc21

2002073741

Manufactured in the United States of America
Dover Publications, Inc., 31 East 2nd Street, Mineola, N.Y. 11501

NOTE

The extraordinary range and diversity of the designs in this volume make them an indispensable practical resource for artists and craftspeople. Over 260 striking designs weave infinite variations on such basic geometric shapes as the circle, square, rectangle, octagon, and oval, producing a rich and varied trove of motifs ideal for a wide range of projects, including wallpaper and textile design, packaging, and computer art. Among the designs are a broad spectrum of intricate, interlocking patterns in a variety of shapes and sizes, offering sinuous, stylized vegetal and foliate motifs, interlocking abstracts suggesting Arabic or Celtic art, kaleidoscopic images, patterns resembling optical illusions, and many more. Artists and craftspeople will find here an almost limitless supply of designs for immediate practical use, as well as a permanent reference ideal for suggesting visual ideas and promoting creativity.

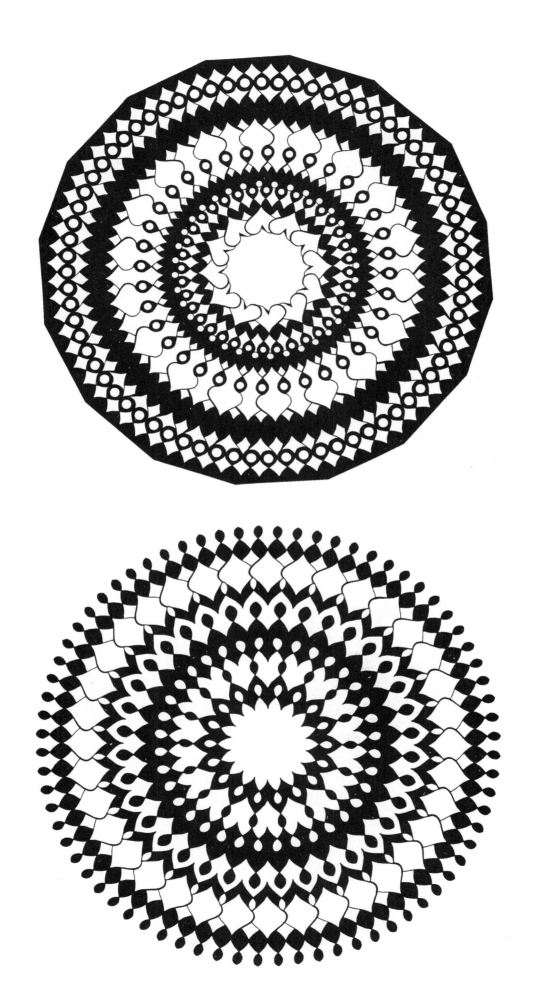

3

4

13

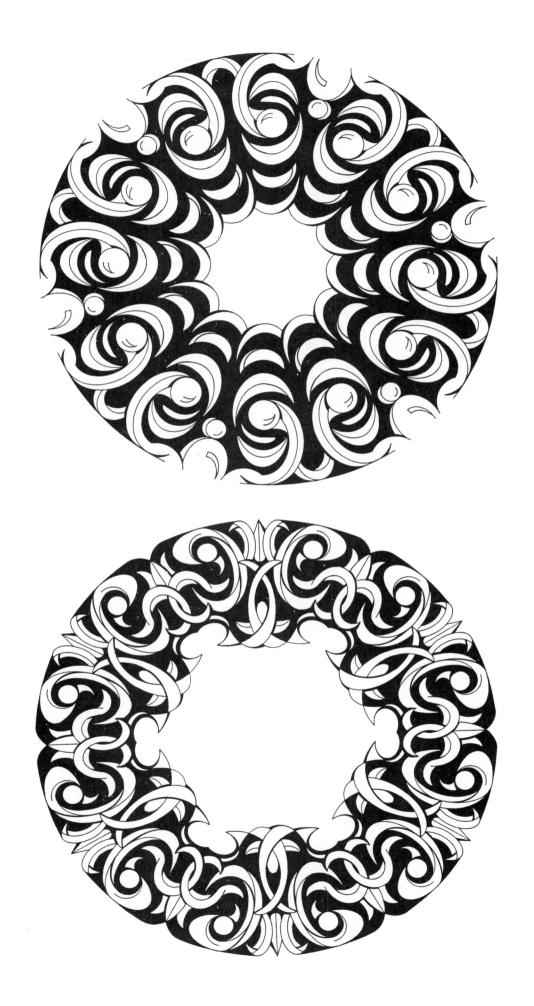

15

18

19

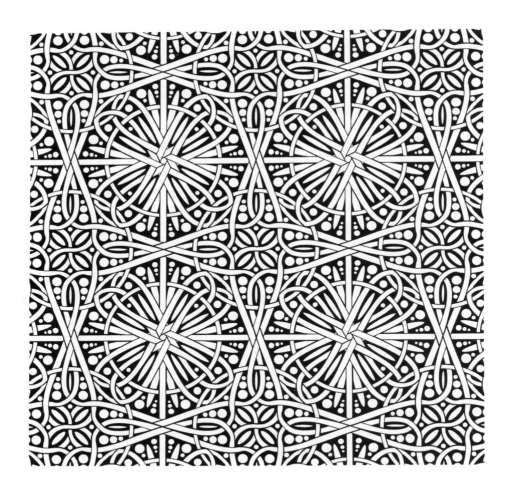

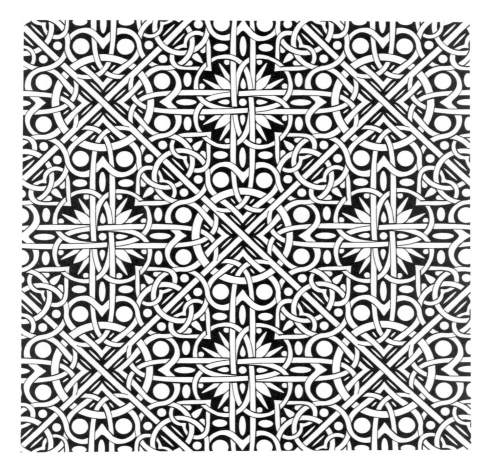

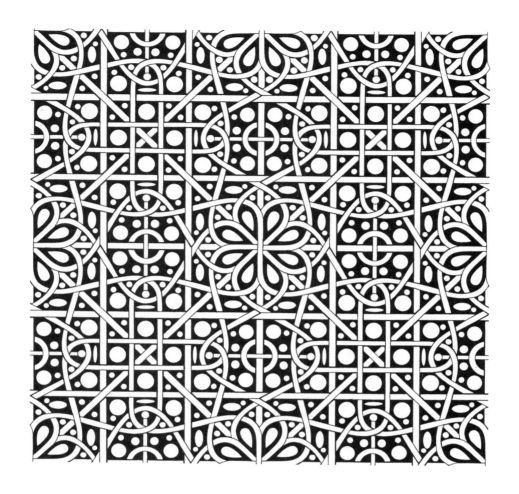

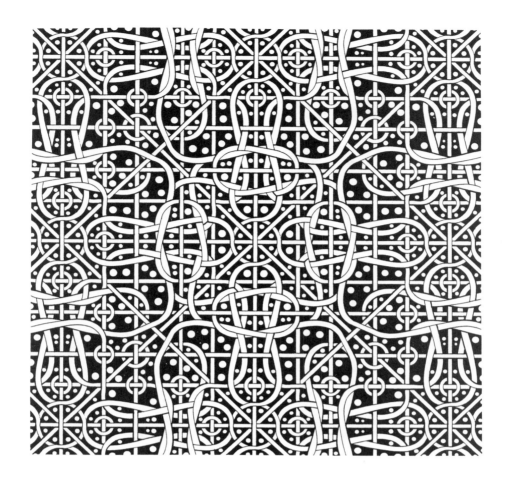

49

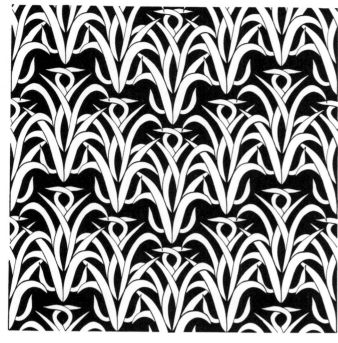

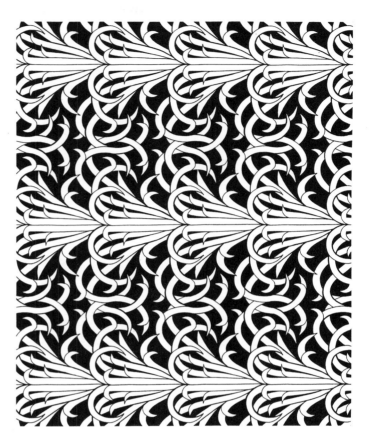

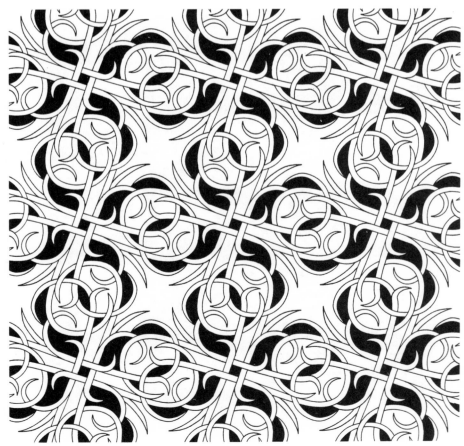

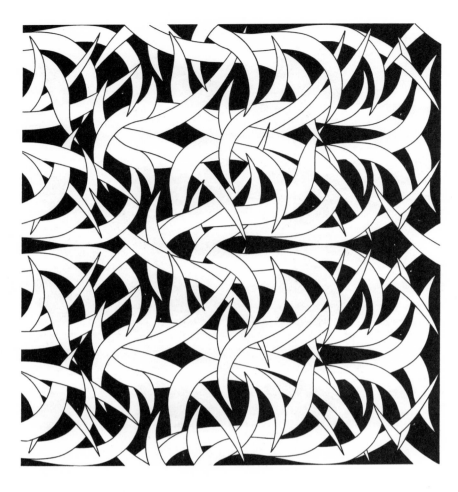

59

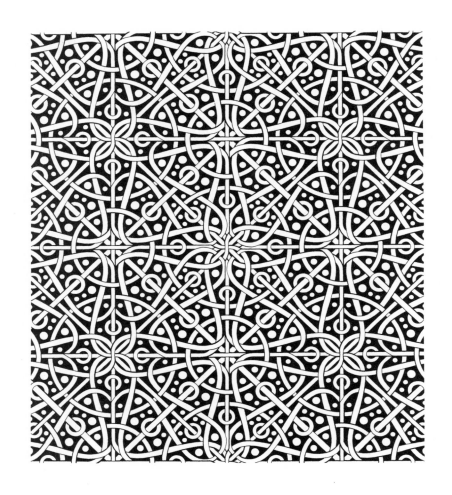

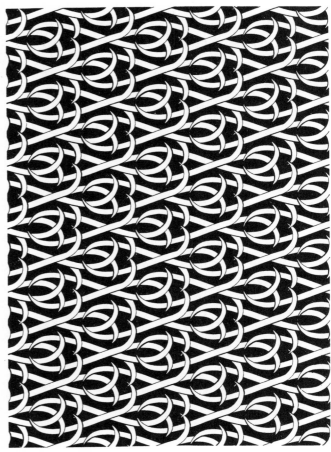

68

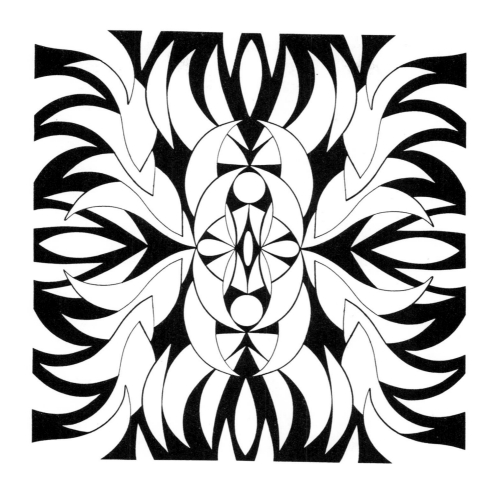

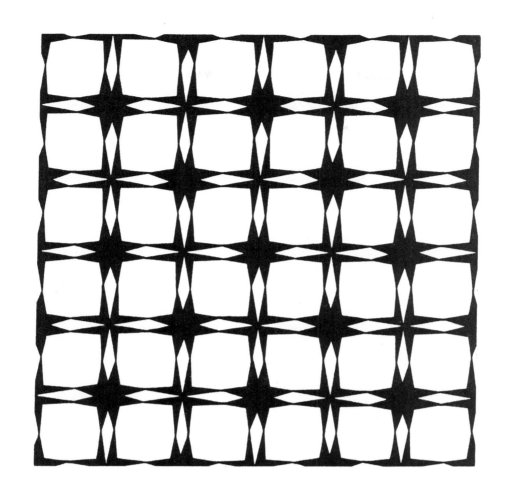

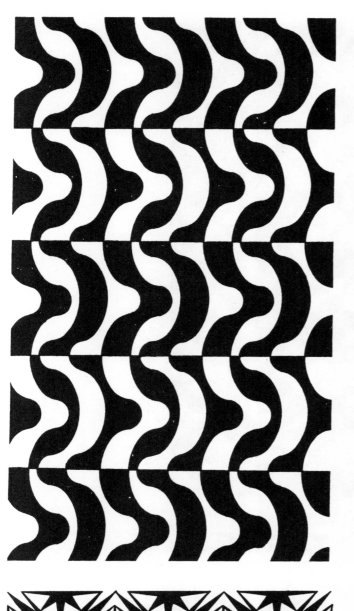

74

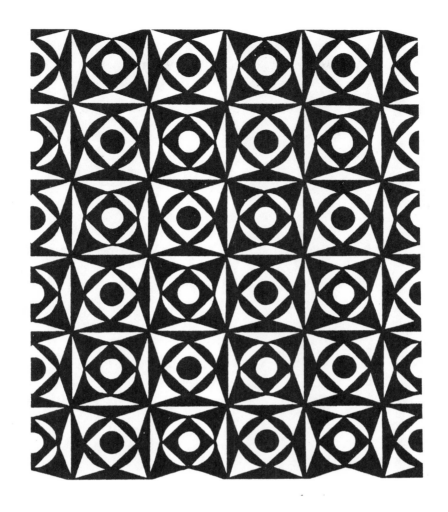

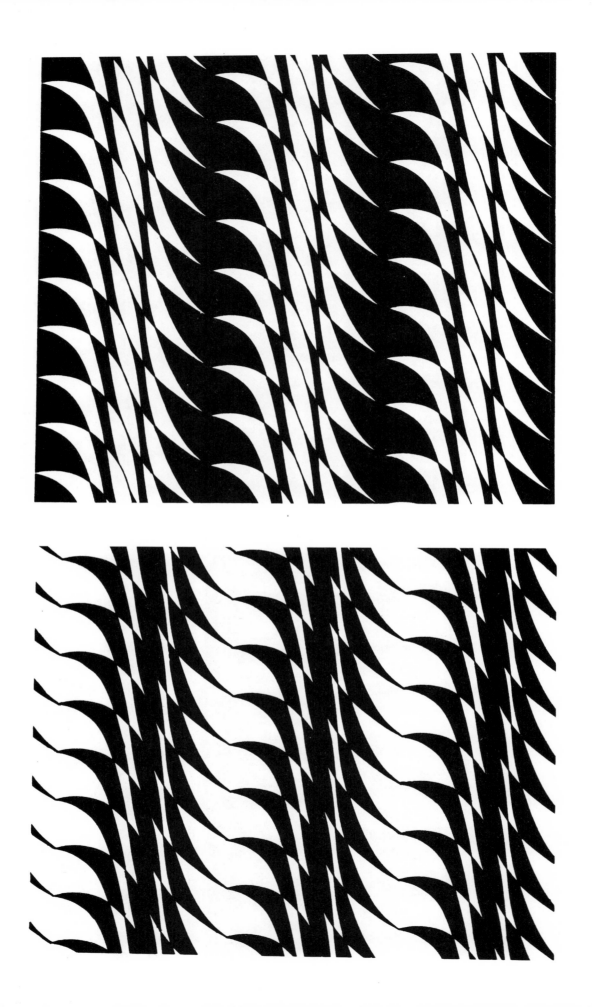

84

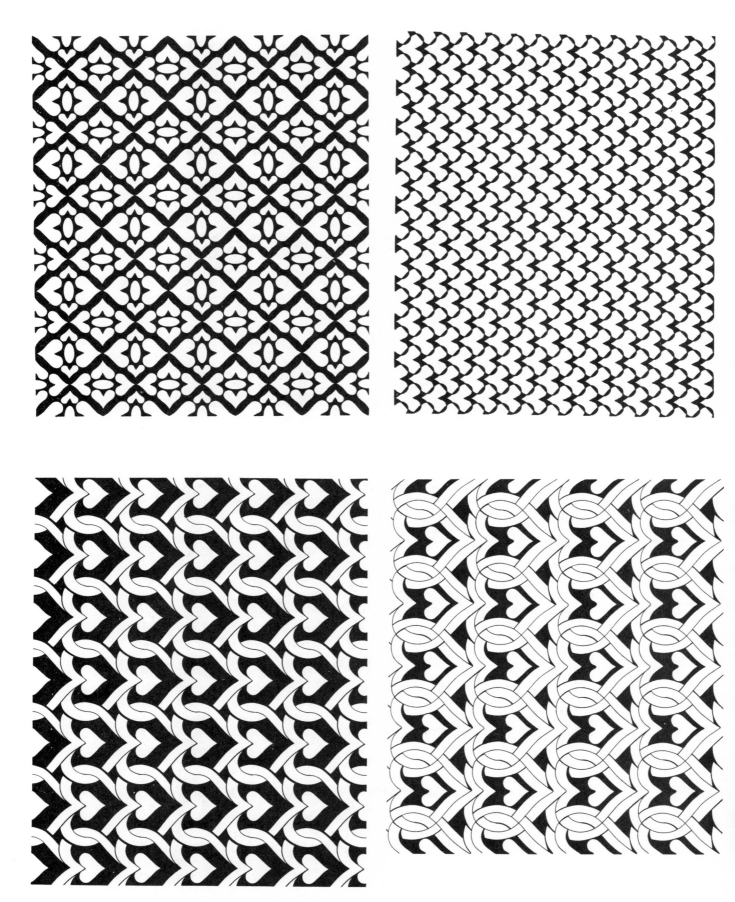

89

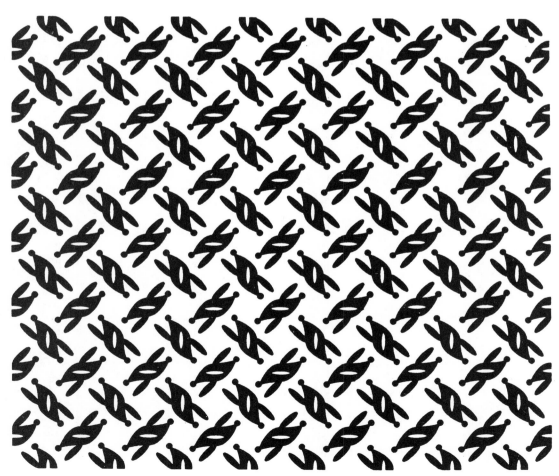

94

99

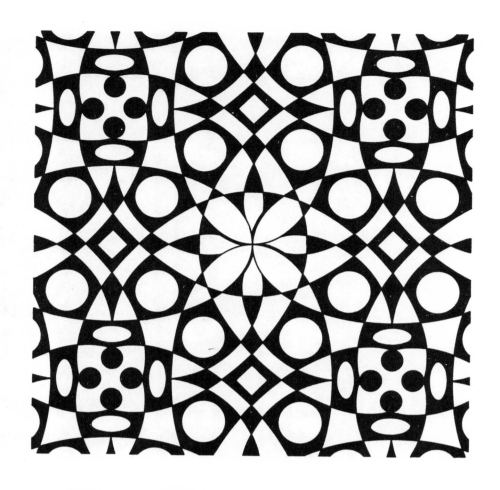

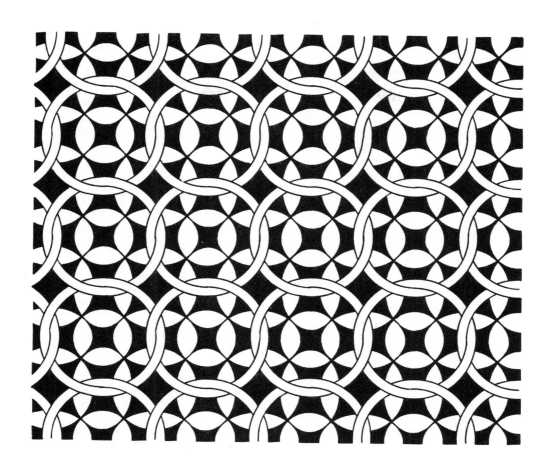

103

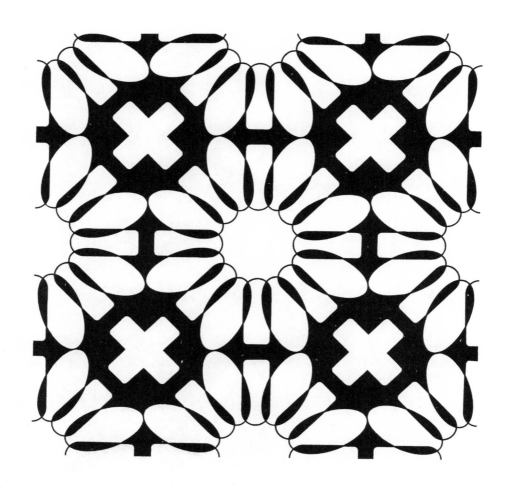

105

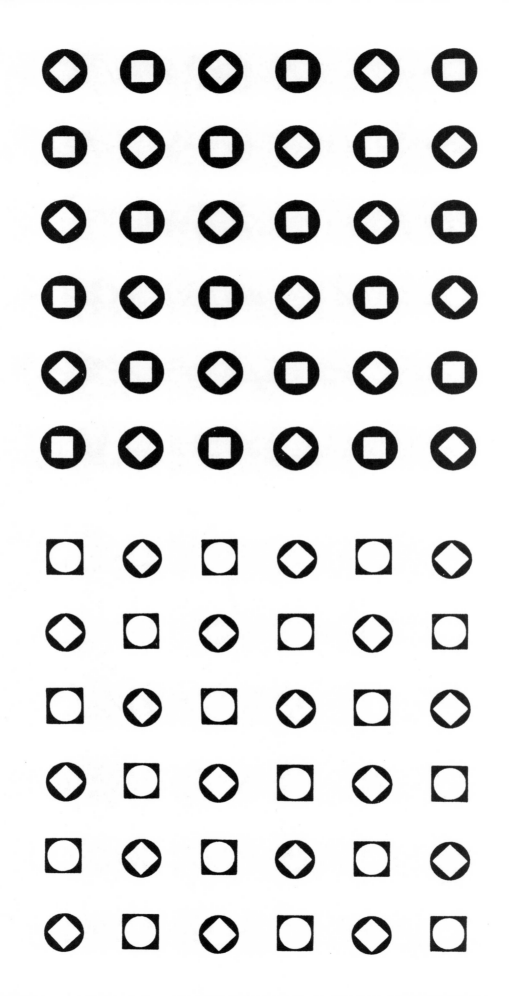

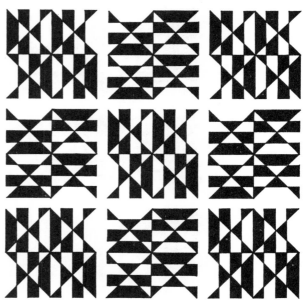

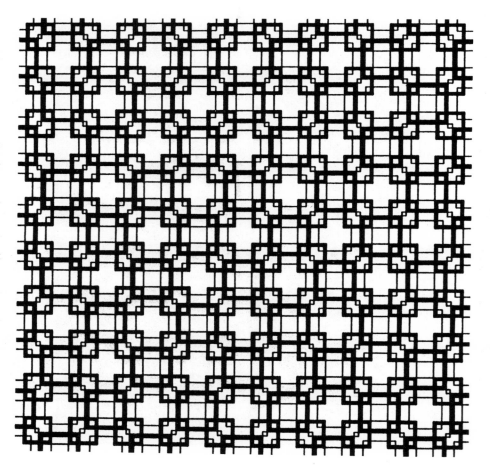

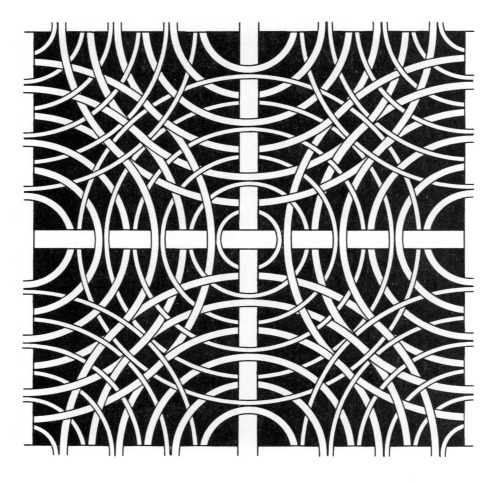

111

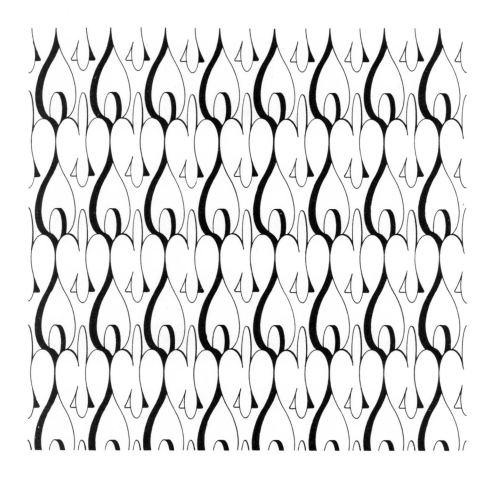